AF268688

Heart Speaks

5: Mother Earth

poems and drawings by

Kathleen Quigley

Heart Speaks Press
Cambridge, Massachusetts 2021

Author photo: Karen Micciulla
Book design: Jonathan Weinert

Printed in the United States of America
First Edition

ISBN 13: 978-1-7373072-1-1

Heart Speaks Press
27 Grozier Road
Cambridge, MA 02138

kathleenquigley.com

Contents

1 – Heart of the Beech Tree 3

2 – Heart of the Calla Lily 7

3 – Heart of the Fern 11

4 – Heart of the Iris 15

5 – Heart of the Flamingo 19

6 – Heart of the Wild Flower 23

7 – Heart of the Oak 27

8 – Heart of the Cow Parsnip 31

9 – Heart of the Fairy Flower 35

10 – Heart of the Succulent 39

11 – Heart of the Earth's Roots 43

12 – Heart of the Wild Rose 47

These drawings are Heart Energy transmissions which help us

to reconnect to our own heart language

and the universal heart — the One. May this book assist you

in creating an ever expansive heart space in which to live from!

My love to you —

Kathleen

This book is dedicated to the living, divine Mother Earth.

With immense love and gratitude for her daily nurturing of all living

life on this planet. May we learn to care for her as she cares for us.

May we become One.

1

♥

Heart of the Beech Tree

Universal Heart Poem
from the High Heart

I Am the energy of the Beech Tree

I live above and I live below

I am a bridge into perfect balance

I ascend as I descend

In both directions simultaneously

Both directions are important

All directions leads to love, in love and through love.

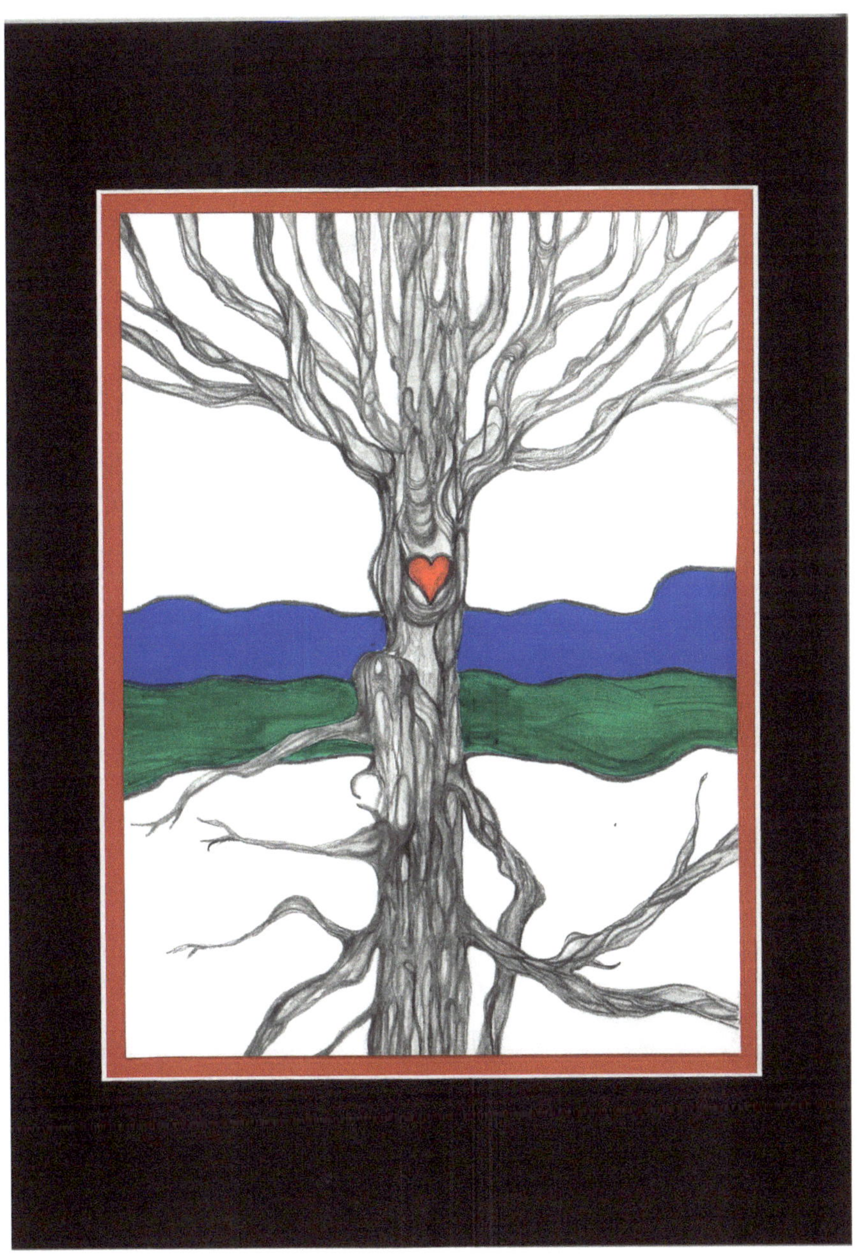

My Heart Wisdom

As above, so below. This is the mirror of Nature. It is important to know the seen world as well as the unseen world. We live in both worlds, as they are connected and reveal different aspects of our divine diamond light existence. All Nature is a mirror unto itself. You are part of Nature. See yourself in the mirror of Nature. Nature is a true reflection of your being. Be the Nature that you were born to be.

2

♥

Heart of the Calla Lily

Universal Heart Poem
from the High Heart

I reflect resurrection

Die to your pictures of who you think you are

Die to who you have been told you are

Rise up in the truth of yourself

Know you are one with All

Rise up in your True Nature

Rise up in Me

Rise up with Me

Rise up through Me

Be your True Nature

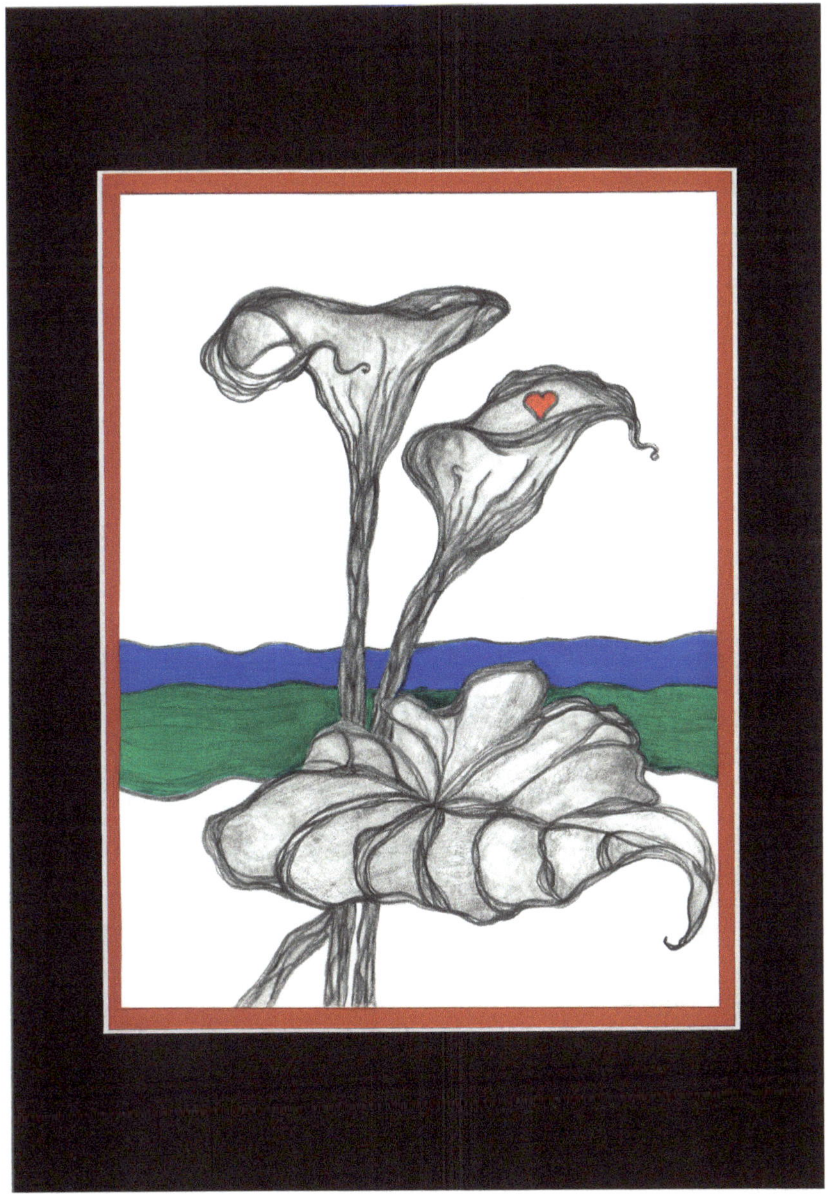

My Heart Wisdom

I Am the Resurrection. I Am the Life. We are in a fluid state of dying and resurrecting. This is the cycle of life and it contains the circles of both birth and death. Look, we see it all around us and yet we ignore it. Every living being is in the process of dying and becoming something new. It is time to embrace our dying. It is time to embrace our resurrecting. One can not happen without the other. Both processes are sacred and part of the life cycle. One can not truly Live until one dies to that which they believe they are. Know your truth and cherish the falling away as well as the resurrecting. It is through death that we truly begin to live.

3

♥

Heart of the Fern

Universal Heart Poem
from the High Heart

I Am the energy of the wild green growth

I breathe

I expand

I grow

Wild is my Nature

Alive I sing

To All

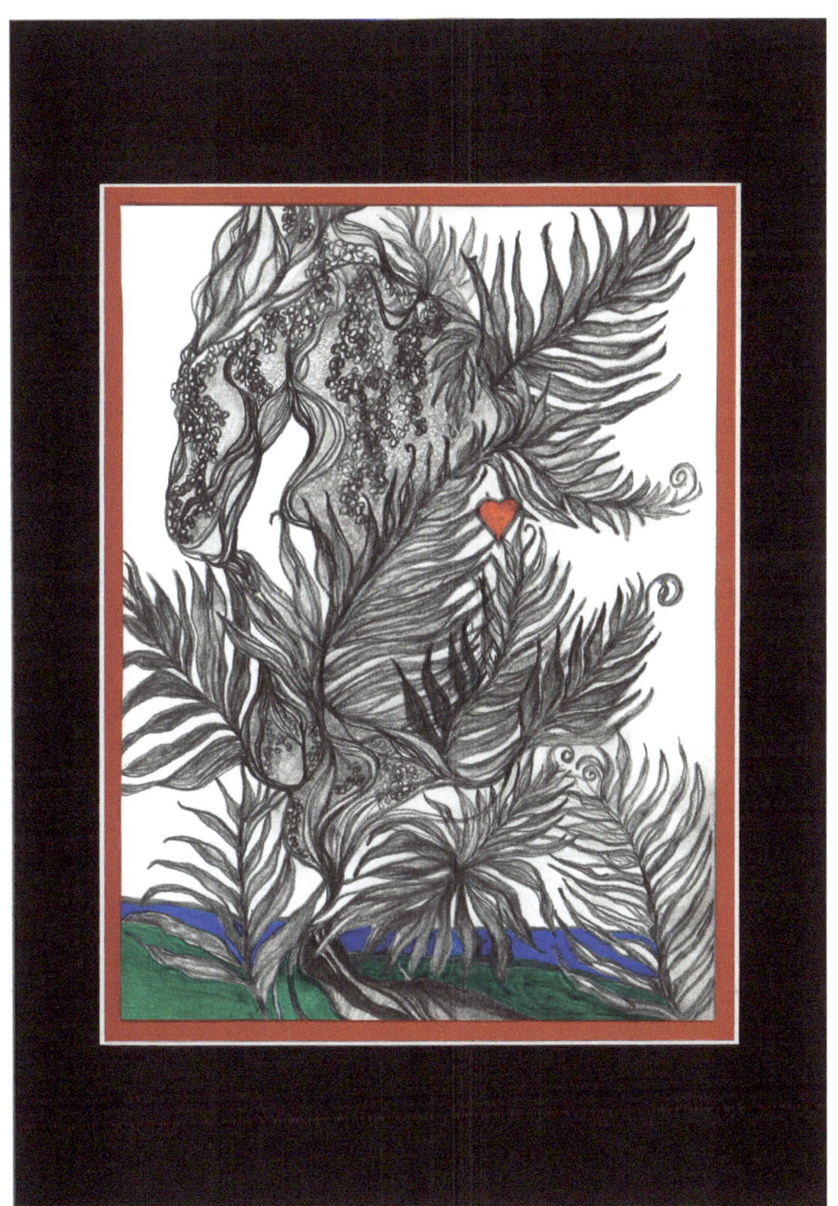

My Heart Wisdom

Can you hear the song of Mother Earth? Listen. . . . It is wild and free. Can you hold it in your heart and begin to sing along? Try...Can you be the wild green growth of Mother Earth? Freedom is calling . . . will you answer? Sing out loud and hear your song of freedom. It is your unique song blended in with the song of life. Will you start to sing along? What is your unique, wild, joyous song?

4

♥

Heart of the Iris

Universal Heart Poem
from the High Heart

I Am the living energy of the Iris

Rising up through the Earth

To greet each and everyone

With the energy of the sacred three

The design is mirrored in all that is living

Embody your true design

Be one in three

Be one in Me

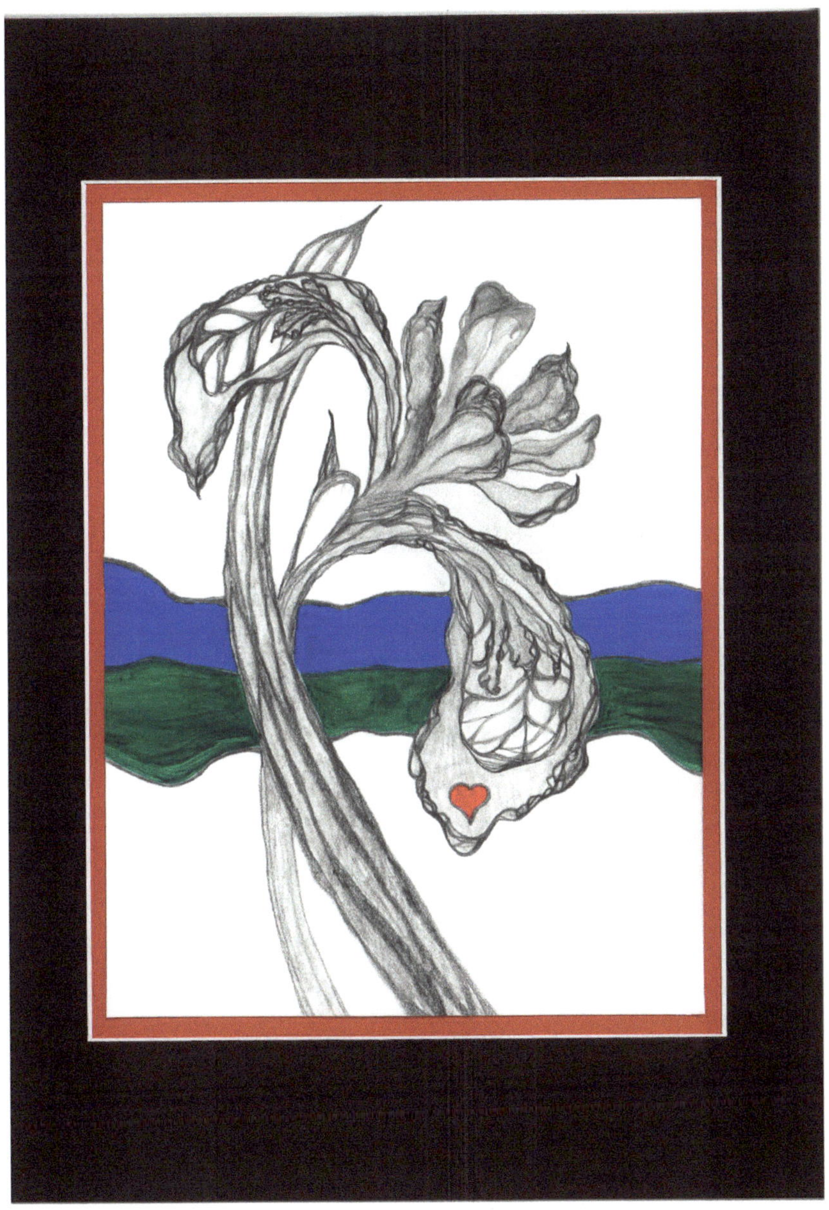

My Heart Wisdom

I am here to remind us of our universal design, the design of life. We are, each living being, designed in the Sacred One through the Sacred Three. These are our sacred roots. This is our divine heritage. This is how our divine DNA is structured. Know this and live your truth always. Know the power of three. Be one in three. . . . Live free!

5

♥

Heart of the Flamingo

Universal Heart Poem
from the High Heart

I Am the energy of love in flight

Love standing alone

Love standing together

Love multiplied and never divided

Stand with me in love

And multiply

Fly with me into a world of love

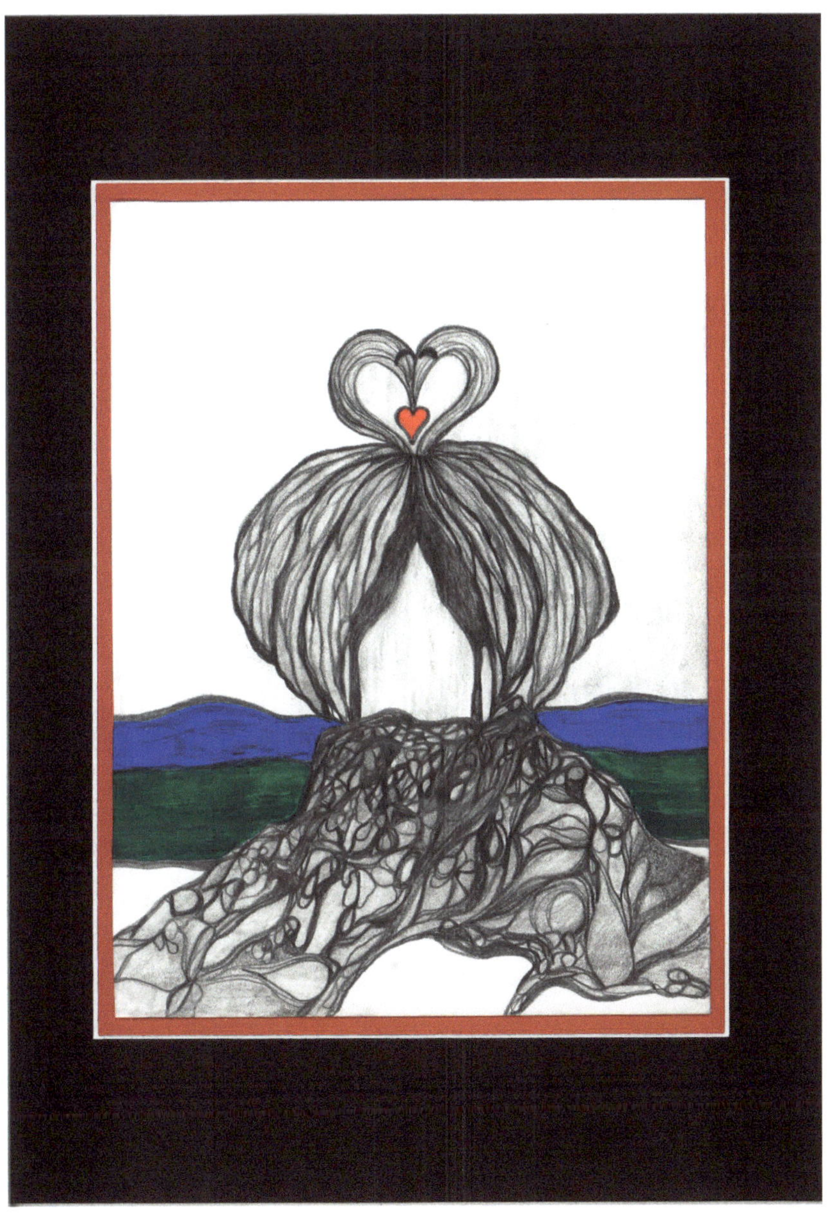

My Heart Wisdom

I am the bird of love and compassion. Pink is the color I become as my love and compassion grows within. It manifests in the outside world to remind you of your true nature. We are all born with the knowing of unconditional love and compassion. Now we must reawaken to our truest nature. The nature of unconditional love for ourselves and for one another. If you can love yourself unconditionally then you will love all life unconditionally. This is our truest state. If you have compassion for yourself, you will have compassion for all. This is our truth.

6

♥

Heart of the Wild Flower

Universal Heart Poem
from the High Heart

I Am the energy of the Wild Flower

I grow wild

I grow free

I sow seeds of freedom on this Earth

Follow my lead to your true nature

Wild and free

Manifest it now

Be Free!

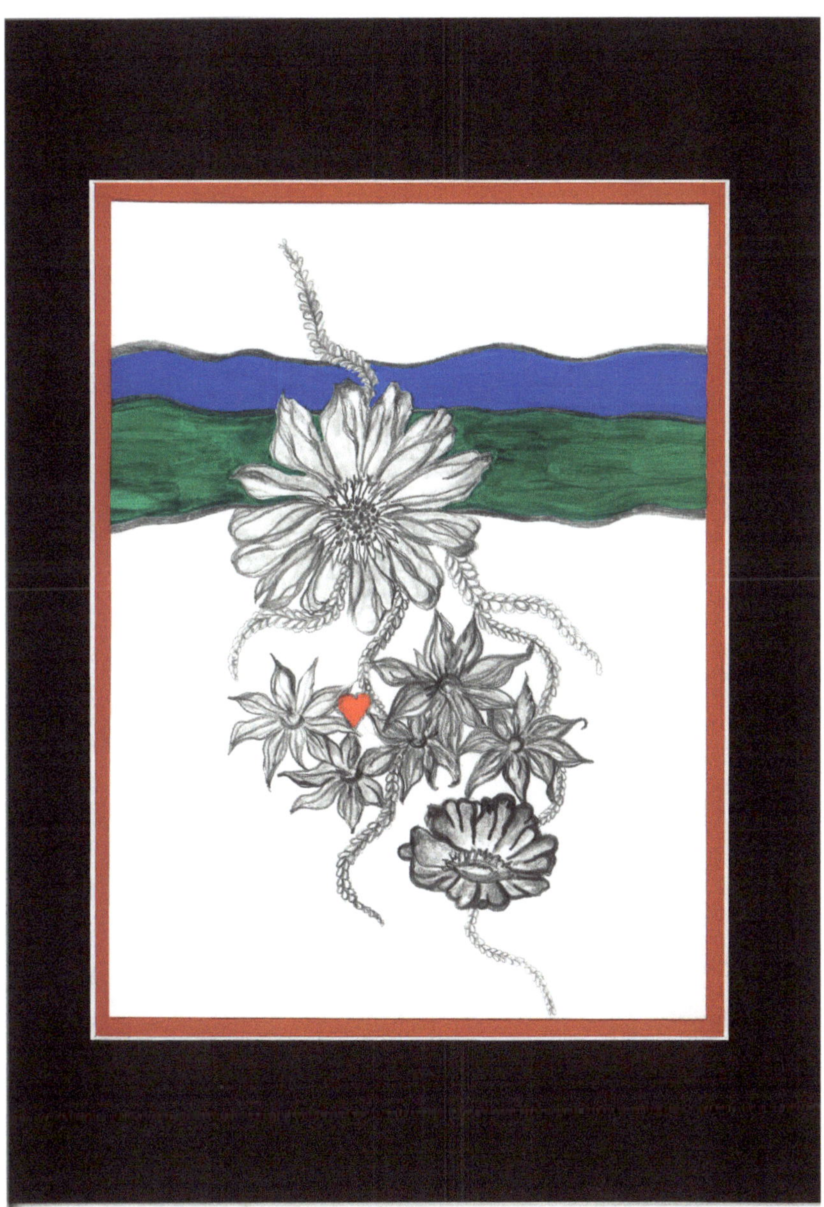

My Heart Wisdom

My wish is freedom for all. My seeds scatter this Earth plane sewing freedom into the soil. Into your soil of your soul. Plant my seeds deep within your heart and water them daily with the songs of freedom. Sing to the heavens, let your soul rejoice in the music of Mother Nature. Let yourself grow like the wild flower. Be Alive! Connect to the music of the spheres and dance with joyous abandonment. Let go and be free.

7

♥

Heart of the Oak

Universal Heart Poem
from the High Heart

I Am the energy of the mighty Oak

My energies permeate this earthly plane with strength and

wisdom

Stand strong in your roots

Know thyself

Love thyself

Connect to the wisdom of the ages

Rise up to the Heavens rooted strongly into the Earth

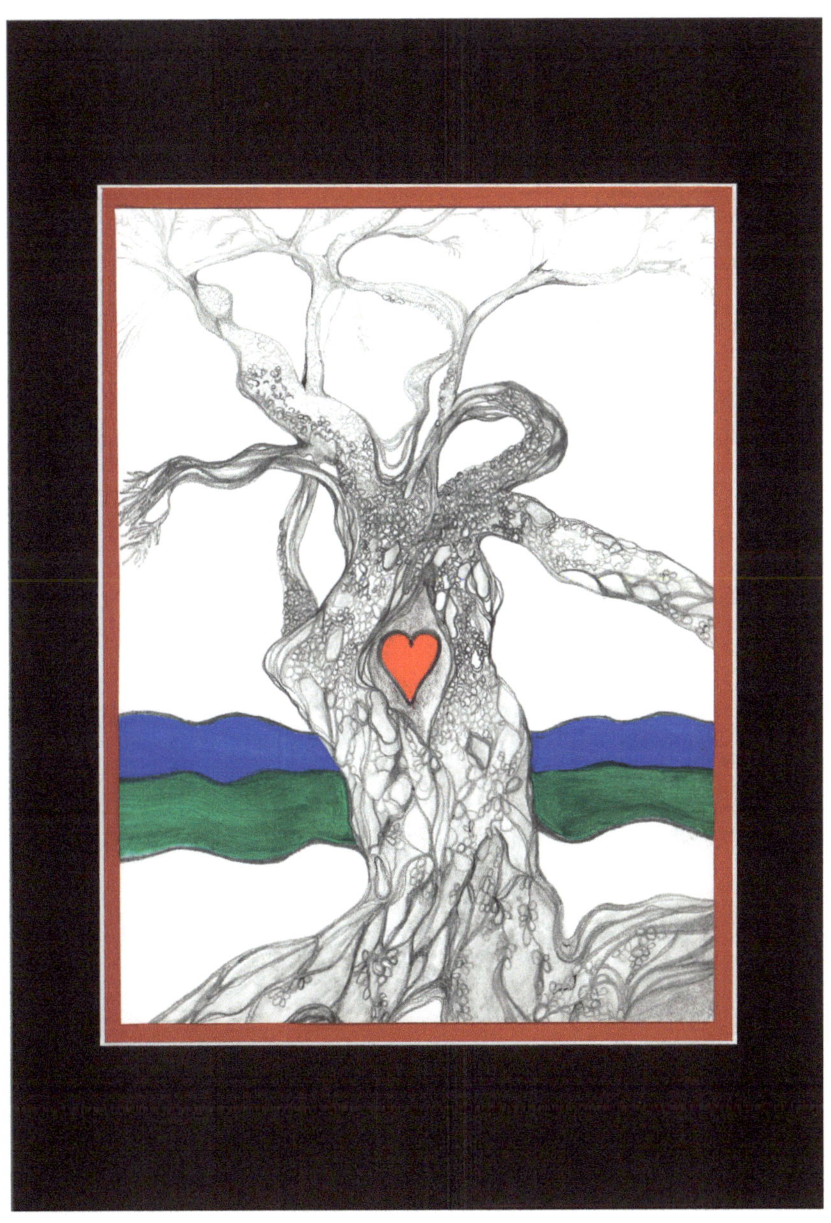

My Heart Wisdom

I Am a mighty force as you are a mighty force. I Am here to mirror my strength and wisdom to you. Know your treeness now. Begin to feel the strength within yourself which allows you to speak your inner wisdom. It is now time to speak up. It is time to root deeply within yourself and find your inner wisdom. Trust yourself and trust the golden flow within. Stand next to me and feel my strength, hear my wisdom and know it is within you. Use me to remind you. I Am here for you. Let us walk together hand in hand, heart to heart.

8

♥

Heart of the Cow Parsnip

Universal Heart Poem
from the High Heart

I Am the energy of the Starry Worlds

I hold star light on this Earthly plane

Facets of light shine from every tiny bud

Star within star

Light within light

Living

Breathing

Alive

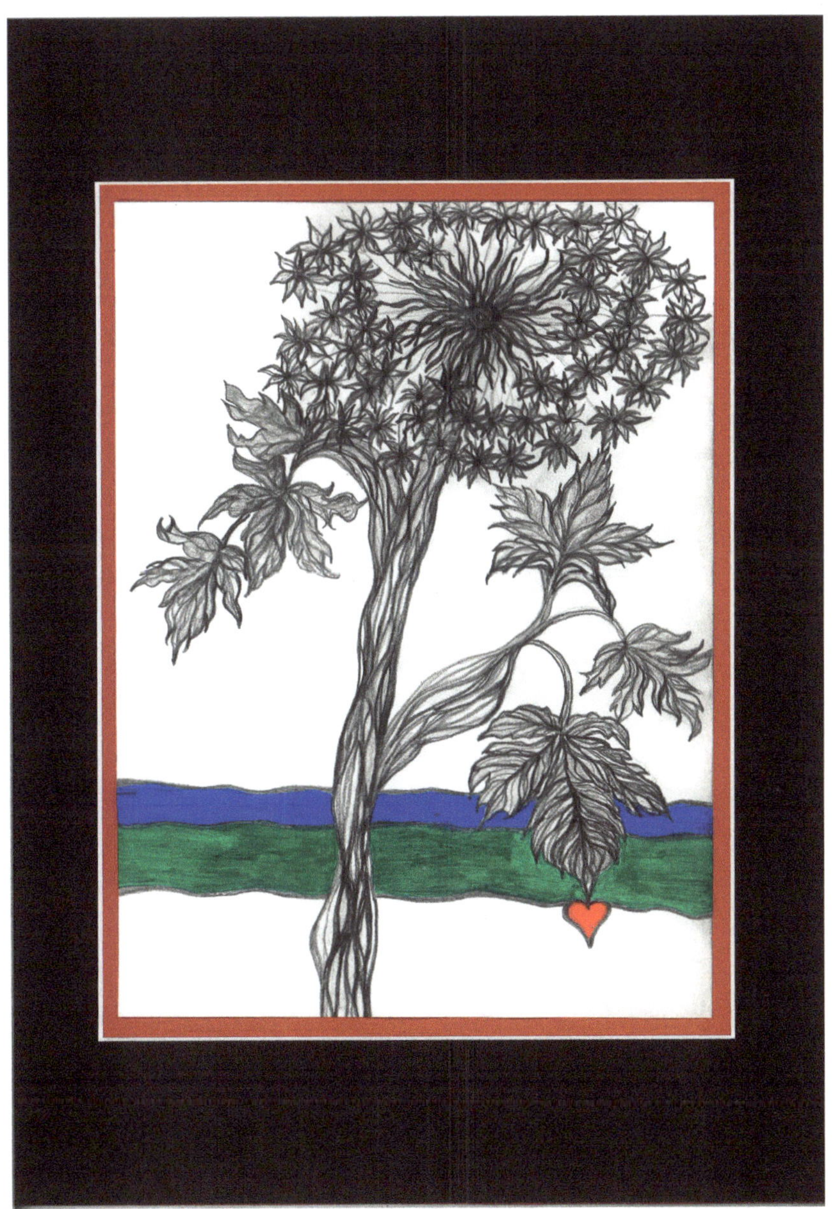

My Heart Wisdom

We are each living, breathing facets of light reflecting back the light from above. Reflecting the light from within. Reflecting to each other, reflecting above, reflecting below, reflecting all around. Sparkles of light reflecting the beauty of Nature. Reflecting the beauty of life itself. Look around, can you see the sparkles? Let the world begin to shimmer its light and drink it in. Star light to star light, begin to shine brighter! Open your heart to the light within and begin to shine brightly. Bring in the light daily, pump out the light daily, continue the circle of light. This is our divine birth right, we are born to shine. We are the light of this world.

9

♥

Heart of the Fairy Flower

Universal Heart Poem
from the High Heart

I Am the energy of the Fairies

The realm of magic and delight

You have forgotten Me

I never forget you

It is time to remember Me again

Step into the magic and begin to see Me

Feel Me

Feel your magic

See Me

See the magic

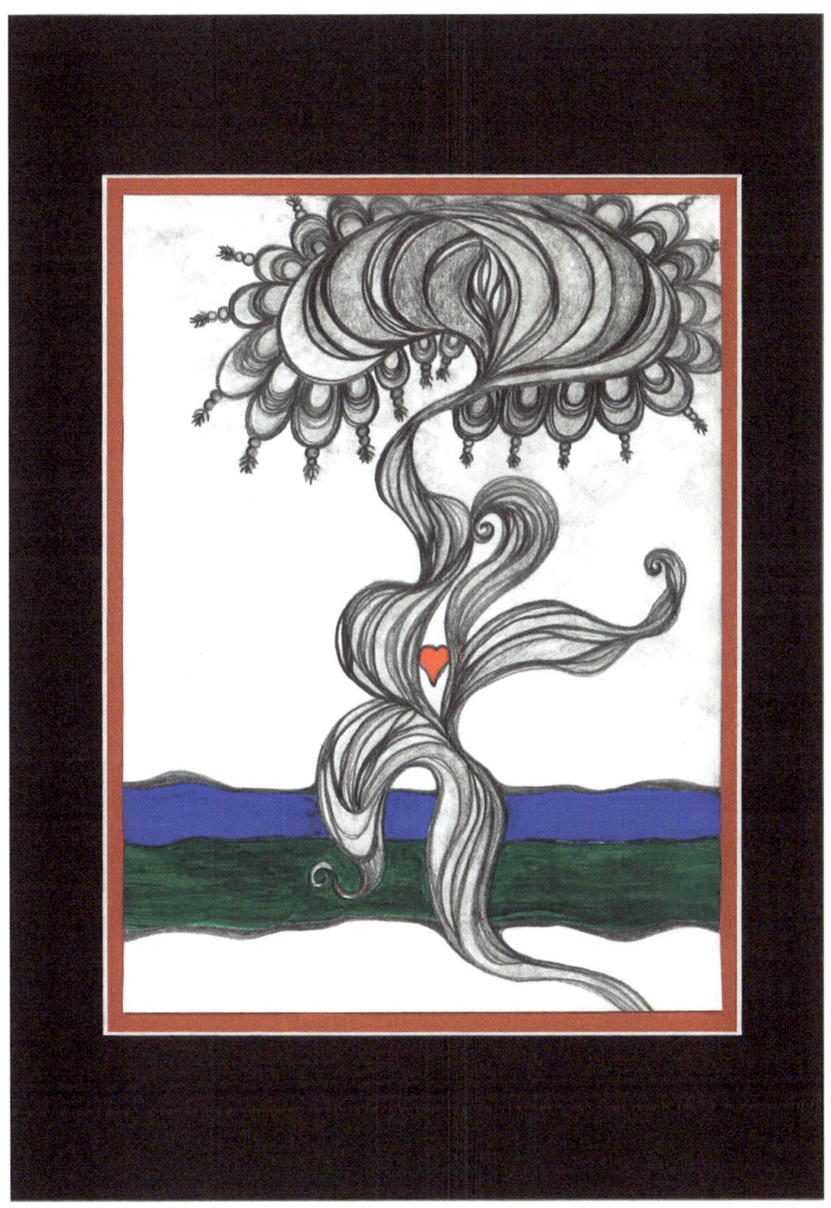

My Heart Wisdom

I Am the energy of magic and delight. I dance into your heart, allow me in. I sing into your heart, sing me in. You have forgotten the realms of magic on this Earth and it is time to remember. Remember you live within a magical Earth plane where all possibilities exist. This is what the world of nature is showing you constantly. Open the eyes of your heart and look into nature and sense the possibilities. Listen for, see, smell and taste the magic all around you. Let your senses come alive. It's all right in front of you. Open your heart to the magic and be amazed, be surprised! Live in the delight daily!!

10

♥

Heart of the Succulent

Universal Heart Poem
from the High Heart

I Am the energy of Flow

Look into my center

See the world within worlds existing

Step into the Infinite

Feel the flow of the worlds

Within You!

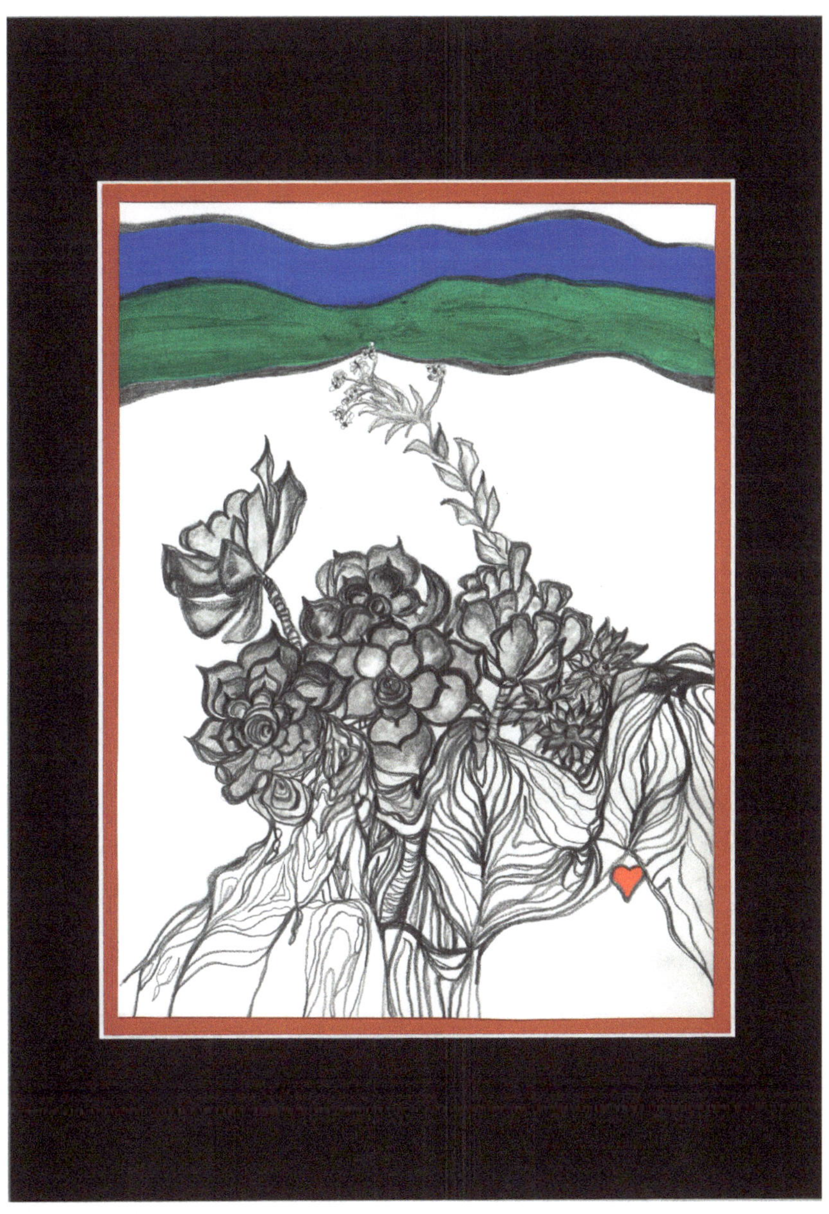

My Heart Wisdom

I Am the energy of flow. I know the preciousness of Divine Flow. I thrive because of this understanding. I Am sustained by the divine Mother Earth allowing all of her blessings in. Allowing her flow to sustain me with all I need and returning that which is no longer needed is the divine flow of life. I mirror this flow in nature and this flow is mirrored in all worlds. It is the Infinite Divine Flow. Explore the infinite within yourself. See the world within worlds and know the Infinite within. Feel the Divine Flow within.

.

11

♥

Heart of the Earth's Roots

Universal Heart Poem
from the High Heart

I Am the energy of connection

I connect all life

I provide nourishment and flow

Root yourself in Me

Connect to the flow of life sustaining nourishment

You are thirsty

Drink from my flow

Connect to the living life source of Mother Earth

Be nourished

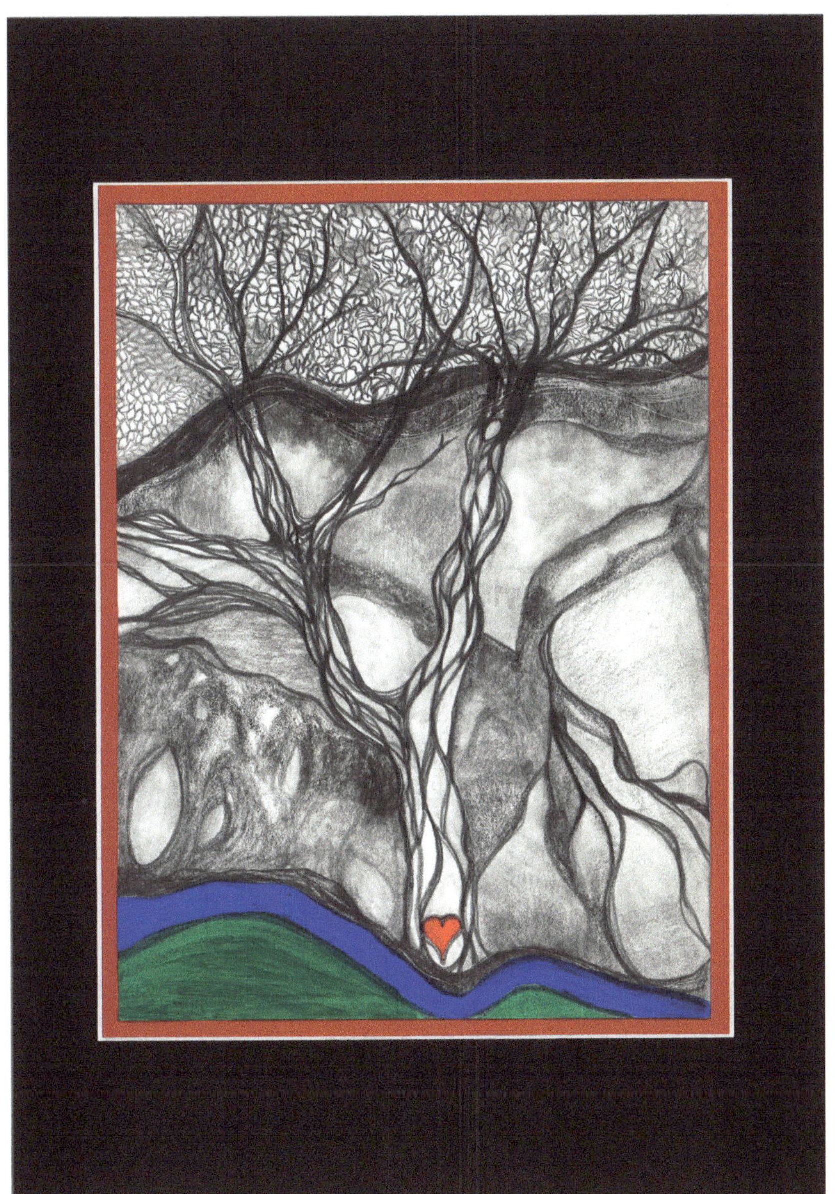

My Heart Wisdom

I Am the nourishment you are seeking. Connect within, connect without. I provide life sustaining, life healing unconditional love. Begin to feel your divine life force from within. Sit in the knowing of your divine connection and feel the flow of the Oneness throughout your physical body and beyond. Let go to the living Life force. Know you are connected to the Life force all around and be in it. Let everything else disappear. Resurrect and be Life. Live your most expanded life now.

.

12

♥

Heart of the Wild Rose

Universal Heart Poem
from the High Heart

I Am the energy of the Sacred Diamond Heart

The Divine Feminine of this Earth plane

I Am the Diamond Beauty Way

Follow me and radiate your love

Open to the rose of your heart

And radiate your love

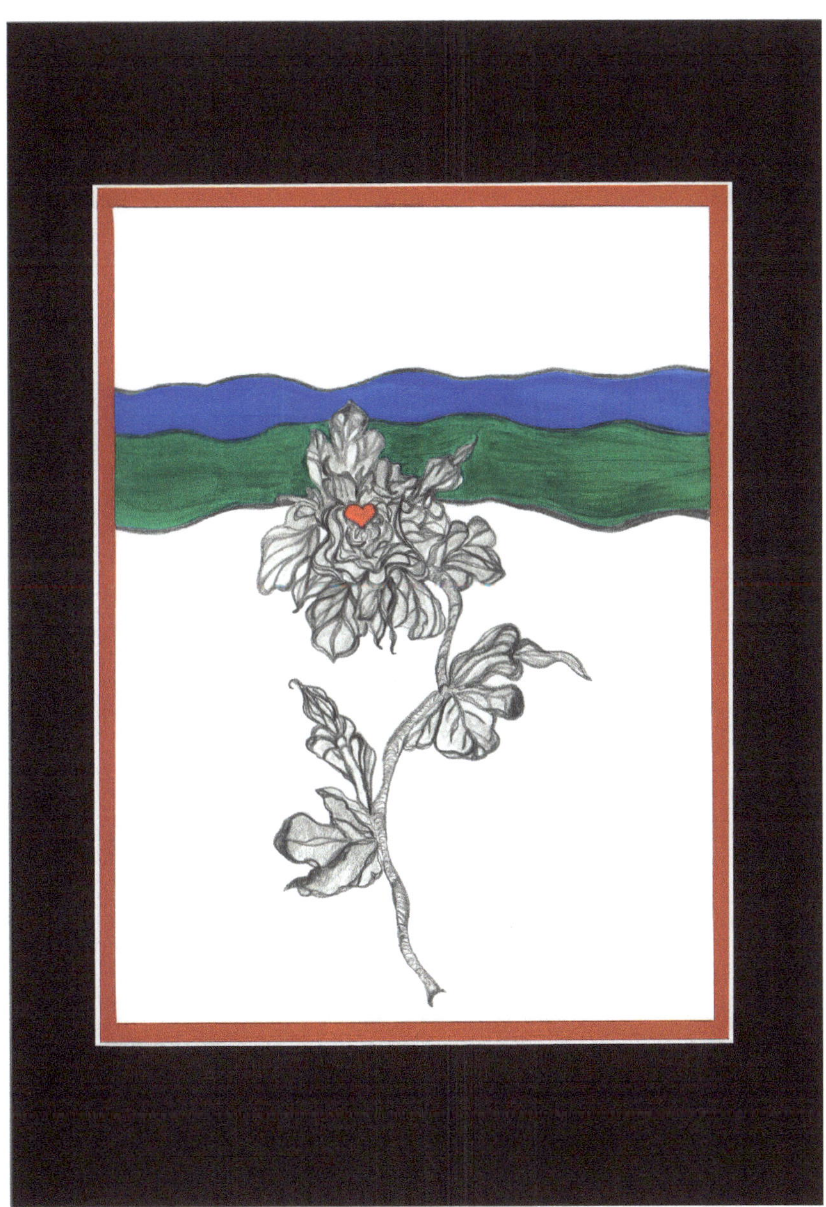

My Heart Wisdom

I Am the energy of Divine Feminine love and beauty. You still don't understand my full potential however you can feel it when you look into a rose. I Am the blueprint of the Divine Feminine. Meditate daily on the Rose. Surround yourself with her beauty. Fall into the Rose and let it absorb all of you through your divine heart space. Let intuition guide you now. Little by little you will become the living rose, happily sustained in you full divine knowing. You are a living part of the Divine Rose Sisterhood. We welcome you!

.

Acknowledgments

I wish to thank Jonathan Weinert whose kindness and
support enables the publishing of the *Heart Speaks* books.
I wish to thank all those who strive to live in oneness with
all life and help nourish Mother Earth, especially Sr. Patricia
Rollinger and the Cuvilly Arts and Earth Center in Ipswich,
MA. To the town of Mendocino, CA, where the beauty
of Nature inspired the drawings and writings in this book.
To all the caretakers of the Earth, I thank you and pray we
follow in your sacred footsteps. My love and gratitude to my
many friends and family whose love and support nourish
me daily. To the Divine High Heart — everlasting and
unconditional love!

About the Artist

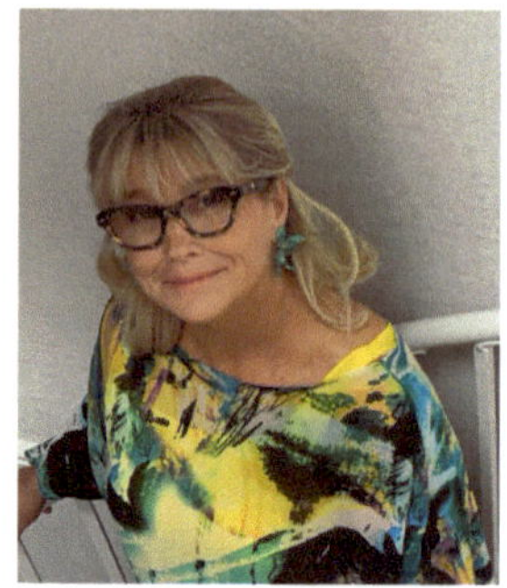

Kathleen Quigley is an artist inspired by the beauty

of nature within and without. She is passionate about

the creative process and its boundless avenues

of communication. You can view her work and contact her

at kathleenquigley.com